Just for Today

To Papu,
brother of my soul

First published in the United States in 2015 by
Eerdmans Books for Young Readers,
an imprint of Wm. B. Eerdmans Publishing Co.
2140 Oak Industrial Dr. NE
Grand Rapids, Michigan 49505
P.O. Box 163, Cambridge CB3 9PU U.K.

www.eerdmans.com/youngreaders

Originally published in Italy in 2011 under the title
Solo Per Oggi
by Edizioni San Paolo s.r.l.,
Piazza Soncino, 5 - 20092 Cinisello Balsamo (Milano), Italy

© 2011 Edizioni San Paolo s.r.l.
English language translation © 2015 Laura Watkinson

Manufactured at Toppan Leefung in China

22 21 20 19 18 17 16 15   9 8 7 6 5 4 3 2 1

ISBN 978-0-8028-5461-2

A catalog record of this book is available
from the Library of Congress.

FSC
www.fsc.org
MIX
Paper from
responsible sources
FSC® C104723

Just for Today

by

SAINT JOHN XXIII

Illustrated by Bimba Landmann

EERDMANS BOOKS FOR YOUNG READERS

GRAND RAPIDS, MICHIGAN • CAMBRIDGE, U.K.

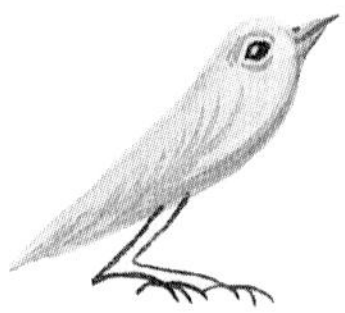

As a child taking his first communion,
seven-year-old Angelo Roncalli declared,
"I want always to be good to everyone."
Years later, he would go on to become beloved Pope John XXIII
and eventually would even be canonized. But throughout his life
he never left that first intention behind — and out of it
grew these words, his decalogue for daily living.
This celebration of love and humility
is a wonderful reminder of
the importance
of living each day fully.

Just for today,
I will try to live
for this day alone,

without wishing to solve my life's
problems all at once.

Just for today, I will take great
care of how I present myself:
I will dress simply; I will not
raise my voice; I will be polite
in my manners;

may   2011
1   8   15   22   29
2   9   16   23   30
3   10   17   24   31
4   11   18   25
5   12   19   26
6   13   20   27
7   14   21   28

I will not criticize anyone;
I will not look to improve or discipline
anyone other than myself.

Just for today, I will be happy in the certainty that I was created to be happy, not only in the world to come, but also in this one.

Just for today, I will adapt to
circumstances, without expecting
circumstances to adapt to my wishes.

Just for today, I will devote ten minutes
of my time to sitting in silence
and listening to God,
remembering that, just as food is
necessary for the life of the body,
so silence and listening are necessary
for the life of the soul.

Just for today, I will do a good deed

and tell no one about it.

Just for today, I will do at least one thing I do not enjoy, and if my feelings are hurt, I will make sure no one notices.

Just for today,
I will make a plan:
perhaps I will not follow it perfectly,

but still I will make it. And I
will guard against two evils:
haste and indecision.

Just for today, I will know,
from the bottom of my heart,
no matter how it may seem,

that God cares for me like
no one else in this world.

Just for today, I will have no fears.

In particular, I will not be afraid
to enjoy what is beautiful
and to believe in love.

I can easily do, for twelve hours,
what I would find discouraging
if I thought I had to do
for a lifetime.

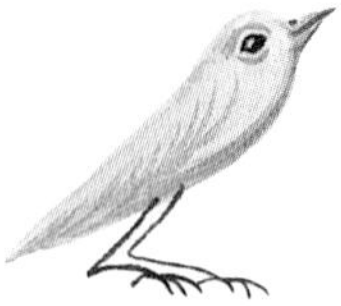

Saint John XXIII

Saint John XXIII served as pope from 1958 until his death in 1963. During his lifetime, he helped save the lives of thousands of Jews fleeing the Holocaust, made a significant effort to resolve the Cuban Missile Crisis, and founded the Second Vatican Council. He was canonized on April 27, 2014.

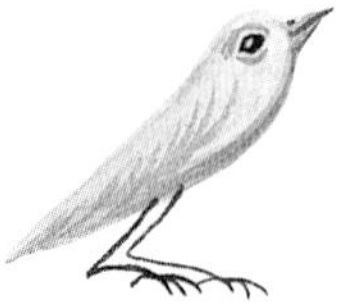

Bimba Landmann

Bimba Landmann has illustrated over a dozen children's books, including *Clare and Francis*, *In Search of the Little Prince*, and *I Am Marc Chagall* (all Eerdmans). Bimba was born in Milan, Italy, where she currently lives with her husband and son.